The Five Dysfunctions of a Team

By Patrick Lencioni

Key Takeaways, Analysis & Review

By Instaread

Please Note

This is a key takeaways and analysis.

Copyright © 2015 by Instaread. All rights reserved worldwide. No part of this publication may be reproduced or transmitted in any form without the prior written consent of the publisher.

Limit of Liability/Disclaimer of Warranty: The publisher and author make no representations or warranties with respect to the accuracy or completeness of these contents and disclaim all warranties such as warranties of fitness for a particular purpose. The author or publisher is not liable for any damages whatsoever. The fact that an individual or organization is referred to in this document as a citation or source of information does not imply that the author or publisher endorses the information that the individual or organization provided. This concise summary is unofficial and is not authorized, approved, licensed, or endorsed by the original book's author or publisher.

Table of Contents

OVERVIEW 4

IMPORTANT PEOPLE 6

Key Takeaways 7

ANALYSIS 9

Key Takeaway 1 9

Key Takeaway 2 11

Key Takeaway 3 13

Key Takeaway 4 15

Key Takeaway 5 17

Key Takeaway 6 19

Key Takeaway 7 21

Key Takeaway 8 23

Key Takeaway 9 25

Key Takeaway 10 27

AUTHOR'S STYLE 29

PERSPECTIVE 31

REFERENCES 32

OVERVIEW

Patrick Lencioni's *The Five Dysfunctions of a Team* is about the reasons teams fail to work together for the collective good of an organization and ways to overcome these problems.

There are five dysfunctions that cause teams to fail. These include teams that do not trust each other, teams that do not engage in productive conflict, teams that cannot commit to collective decisions, teams that do not hold each other accountable, and teams that fail to focus on collective goals. The five dysfunctions are all interrelated. When a team falls victim to one of the five dysfunctions, they become vulnerable to the other four.

The initial step in addressing these dysfunctions is to build trust between team members. Once that is done, members will be ready to engage in productive conflict. Since the conflict means they have had a say in collective decisions, they will then be ready to commit to those decisions. Learning to commit to group decisions will make them more open to providing other team members with feedback about how the others are doing. Holding each other accountable, in turn, helps a team focus on collective goals. That is because no team member wants to let other members down, preventing them from reaching the goals.

IMPORTANT PEOPLE

Kathryn Petersen: The new CEO of an underachieving fictional company, DecisionTech, tries to build an executive team that works well together so the company can achieve the results it has failed to attain so far. She lays out the five dysfunctions of a team for her executives and asks them to work with her to build a cohesive team.

The DecisionTech executive team: This is the fictional team of executives that Kathryn Petersen tries to get to work together for the collective good of the company. She turns around most of them, but loses a couple along the way, one who was putting her career over the collective good.

Key Takeaways

1. The first dysfunction of a team is an inability to trust.
2. The second dysfunction of a team is fear of engaging in conflict.
3. The third dysfunction of a team is lack of commitment to team decisions.
4. The fourth dysfunction of a team is unwillingness to hold other team members accountable.
5. The fifth dysfunction of a team is the inability to focus on collective goals as opposed to individual goals.
6. A leader can use various techniques to help build trust among team members.
7. To engage in productive conflict, team members must first understand what productive conflict is.
8. The main ingredient for team member commitment is for every member of a team to have a say in the decision making process.

9. It is often necessary to hold team members accountable for their shortcomings to force them to be better team players.
10. Ways to overcome an inability to focus on collective goals include making the goals public and rewarding only those behaviors and actions that lead to achieving those goals.

ANALYSIS

Key Takeaway 1

The first dysfunction of a team is an inability to trust one another.

Analysis

The main obstacle to a team building trust is that many people are unwilling to be vulnerable with each other. That is, they are unwilling to show their strengths and their weaknesses. It is only natural that many people fear that any admission of weakness will be used against them some day. For example, a past mistake or vulnerability could be used to deny someone a promotion.

Instaread on The Five Dysfunctions of a Team

Some organizations deliberately foster a culture of distrust among their executive team members, believing incorrectly that it will deliver better results. A major newspaper chain used to do that by pitting key team members against each other. Typically, the CEO of one of the chain's papers would hold one-on-one meetings with three members of the executive team at which he would announce that a promotion will be available soon and the three invitees are the forerunners for the job. The CEO may think that pitting these executives against each other will generate the best results for the company since each of the executives will be working hard to prove themselves. But the CEO is actually putting an emphasis on the results of the three executives' individual departments, not the entire company. This kind of scenario usually sets in motion a bitter rivalry among the three executives, who will not work with each other in fear of giving their rivals the upper hand. And, although those executives' departments may show great results, the company's results as a whole may be disappointing. Another downside of pitting executives against each other is that when one finally gets the promotion, those who were passed over often leave, costing the company top talent.

Key Takeaway 2

The second dysfunction of a team is fear of engaging in conflict.

Analysis

Productive conflict is the kind of conflict where ideas are debated openly so that all sides of an issue can be explored with the goal of making the best group decision possible when addressing the issue. Teams that are unable to trust each other will not engage in productive conflict. Instead of voicing their opinions, many people will hold back for fear of offending others or being seen as the odd person out.

One reason that many team members are reluctant to engage in conflict in a team setting that could generate the best decisions possible is that most organizations also tell their employees that conflict in the workplace is inappropriate. Not only do many organizations convey this message, but they also make the ability to get along with others one of the performance standards they use to evaluate employees for pay increases and promotions. After being told that engaging in conflict in the workplace will be counted against them, many employees find it difficult to accept the notion that they should now engage in conflict in a team setting. The leader of a team who wants productive conflict in the team setting needs to explain the difference between personality conflicts and conflict within a team setting. That may help prod reluctant team members toward engaging in the kind of productive conflict the leader wants.

Key Takeaway 3

The third dysfunction of a team is lack of commitment to team decisions.

Analysis

If team members hold back from offering their unfettered views on an issue during a team debate, they will usually not be committed to the final decision the team makes. Since they have not put their mind, heart, and soul into the discussion that precedes the decision or if they oppose the decision the group makes, they will likely not buy into it and try to make it work. If they have expressed their views clearly, and the team decides against them, they are more likely to buy into the team decision.

Much has been written over the years about the advantages of the Japanese management system. One of these advantages is that the system produces a buy-in on key decisions all the way from the lowest ranking employees to the top executives. This is because top executives ask that any important new idea be discussed by everyone in the company before it is adopted. Those at the lowest ranks discuss it first. The discussion moves up the chain step by step among groups of employees until it reaches the executives. By the time the discussion is at the top, the executives know both the pros and cons of going with the idea and employees' consensus on whether it should be adopted. The executives then make a decision. Usually that decision supports the employee consensus that has been reached, but not always. Japanese managers devised this system to obtain buy-in on key decisions. They learned long ago that if employees have their say on an issue, they will buy into a group decision on the issue even if they oppose the decision. Beginning in the 1970s and 1980s, when American companies discovered that Japanese companies were outcompeting them, many adopted Japanese management approaches, including company wide discussions to obtain buy-in [1].

Key Takeaway 4

The fourth dysfunction of a team is unwillingness to hold other team members accountable.

Analysis

When all the members of a team fail to commit to a team decision or plan of action, many are reluctant to hold accountable others whom they view as dropping the ball, or telling other team members that their actions or behaviors are going against the collective good.

Most supervisors, including executives, find it difficult to tell employees in other departments that they are doing something that is counterproductive. Their reluctance stems from that old adage "Don't stick your nose in other people's business." Unless two team members trust each other and are both committed to a common goal, the reaction from the person who is being called out may be argumentative. Word that an employee is overstepping their bounds by second guessing an employee in a different department quickly gets around, causing resentment among employees of the section whose leader was second guessed. This means that one team member holding another accountable at a meeting can be fraught with danger. It takes a very skilled team leader to create an atmosphere where peer-to-peer accountability can occur without generating resentment.

Key Takeaway 5

The fifth dysfunction of a team is an inability to focus on collective goals as opposed to individual goals.

Analysis

There are many individual goals that members of a team can focus on instead of collective results. They include winning company awards or obtaining other recognition, getting a promotion, and building a resume that will let them move to a bigger, more prestigious company. However, these goals do nothing to insure the best company wide results.

Some company leaders have the idea that if every executive on their team do a great job leading their own department, then company wide results will, by extension, be great as well. That is not necessarily the case. Leaders who send that type of message are unwittingly telling executive team members that they should focus on individual results rather than company wide results. This prompts executives in charge of various departments to do whatever it takes to make themselves and their department look good rather than worry about the company as a whole.

Key Takeaway 6

A leader can use various techniques to help build trust among team members.

Analysis

Building trust takes time, but a leader can hasten the process with various techniques. One way to help team members get to know each other is to have each tell the team something unique about their lives. Another is to ask members what is the most important contribution and biggest shortcoming of other team members. Finally, the leader could reveal the results of professionally administered personality profile evaluations of each team member. These offer insight into members' proclivities, behavior, and character.

Outdoor team exercises are another way to build team trust. For example, some team building coaches create a rope obstacle course that a team must negotiate together. Members use their strengths to help each other get through the course as efficiently as possible. The military not only uses obstacle courses to toughen recruits, but also to identify future leaders on the basis of whether they can build team trust. Take officer training, for instance. The instructors watch whether recruits tackle an obstacle course by themselves, not caring whether others make it through, or whether they try to help those who are faltering. The recruit who helps others is deemed a good team player, someone who builds team trust, and thus a good bet for leadership. That is because the person is considered someone who can likely create a team whose members trust each other when carrying out a mission. The main source of conflict in the classic 1984 movie *An Officer and a Gentleman* was a instructor's attempt to prevent a recruit he disliked from graduating Navy officer training. The instructor disliked the fact that the recruit did nothing to try to gain his teammates' trust but instead continually showed that he did not care about them and was all for himself. The movie ended with the recruit becoming a team player.

Key Takeaway 7

To engage in productive conflict, team members must first understand what productive conflict is.

Analysis

Before team members can engage in productive conflict, they must first understand the difference between conflict over ideas and conflict over personal issues. It is not only all right, but necessary for a team to debate ideas because it leads to the company generating the best ideas to act on. It is not all right, however, to engage in mean-spirited personal attacks.

The notion of a team leader asking a member to precipitate conflict at a team meeting would horrify executives who place team harmony above all else. And purposely generating conflict can be fraught with danger. That is because the conflict is usually focused on sensitive issues that are simmering below the surface that team members would rather not address. An example of such an issue is whether the company is doing a good job of hiring and promoting minorities. Race and ethnicity can be an explosive issue, so many people in a company, including executives, would rather not address it in an open forum such as an executive meeting. Yet it does need to be addressed for a company to be fair to all of its employees and to obtain the most out of everyone. And giving the issue attention in a forum where lots of people can offer and debate ideas can lead to ways a company can do a better job of hiring and promoting minorities. The key to having an unfettered debate on such a sensitive topic is for the leader to point out that a debate on the issue is necessary and will lead to a better company.

Key Takeaway 8

The main ingredient for team member commitment is for every member of a team to have a say in the decision making process.

Analysis

The two major obstacles to lack of commitment are a desire to seek group consensus on an issue and fear that a group decision may end up being wrong. Consensus means everyone on a team, or almost everyone, agrees with an idea or approach. This is usually impossible. However, those who oppose a group decision will commit to it if they had a chance to voice their opinion on it. The way to overcome lack of commitment to a decision when some team members fear it will be wrong is for a leader to emphasize that if the decision does turn out to be wrong, it can be scrapped for a new approach.

One of the most cherished phrases a team leader can hear from a team member during a group meeting is: "I don't agree with that approach, but if that is what the rest of you want, I will do my best to make it work." Unfortunately, the corporate world is full of instances of employees who, after being outvoted on an issue, tried to sabotage the group decision. Blatant sabotage would lead to the employee being fired, so that is not the tactic most dissenters use. Rather, they often adopt the group decision halfheartedly, hoping it will fail. When employees who are on the losing end of a group vote on a new approach commit to making it work, a leader can be sure that this means the decision making debate process that the team has established insures that all team members can have their say. That is the main ingredient for commitment, not consensus.

Key Takeaway 9

It is often necessary to hold team members accountable for their shortcomings to force them to be better team players.

Analysis

Holding other team members accountable for their shortcomings in a public setting cannot help but generate discomfort. And the discomfort is universal. It applies to the person who is calling out another team member, the member who is being called out, and everyone watching this exchange. The call out is necessary, however, because its public nature will force faltering team members to try to do better.

Anyone who has been in a team culture where peer-to-peer accountability has never been established can predict what will happen when one team member calls out another at a meeting. No matter how diplomatic the process, the member who is being called out will become angry and defensive. They may not make an open show of anger or defensiveness, but it will be there and other team members will be able to feel it. Often the reputations of both the person making accusations and the person being accused take a hit. Other team members see the person doing the accusing as wrongfully intruding on someone else's turf, as airing dirty laundry in public, and as being either insensitive or a bully. Meanwhile, the person being called out looks bad for letting the team down. A team leader can facilitate peer-to-peer accountability by stressing its importance to team goals, by noting that accusations are about performance, not personal, and stressing that every team member should hold their peers accountable. It is likely to take time for a productive system to evolve, but it can evolve to the benefit of the team and the company.

Key Takeaway 10

Ways to overcome an inability to focus on collective goals include making the goals public and rewarding only those behaviors and actions that lead to achieving the goals.

Analysis

The first step a leader can take to overcome team members' inability to focus on collective goals is to have the team set collective goals that are very specific. The next step is for the leader to emphasize over and over the importance of focusing on collective goals as opposed to individual goals. Collective goals do not have to involve just the bottom line, but can involve other yardsticks, such as the number of new customers.

The reason some team members, even executive team members, can become confused about which goals should be their overriding concern is that goals their bosses set for their performance reports are usually a combination of individual and department wide goals, not company wide goals. Team leaders can help resolve this problem by making sure that performance report goals do a good job of supporting the attainment of company wide goals. Most executives' performance report goals do not conflict with company wide goals. But some individual or department wide goals do a better job of promoting the attainment of company wide goals than others.

AUTHOR'S STYLE

Patrick Lencioni's main literary device in *The Five Dysfunctions of a Team* is storytelling and it is an effective one for getting his points across. Rather than write only about his model of team dysfunctionality, Lencioni writes about how dysfunctions affect those on a team. He does this by creating a fictional company, DecisionTech, and its executive team.

He uses a realistic set of executive team characters, each with their own strengths, weaknesses, and foibles. Anyone who has worked in any organization, can relate to most of the team members as they have seen similar people in their own workplaces. This makes for a realistic portrayal of how the team members act around each other.

Lencioni makes his storytelling even more compelling by building suspense as in a fiction novel about whether Petersen, his fictional CEO, will retain members of the team who appear to be putting their individual careers above the company's collective good. For example, Petersen goes back and forth on whether to retain Michele Bebe, the head of DecisionTech's marketing division, before making a final decision. Much of the time Mikey does things that show she is not a team player. In a few instances, she shows signs she could change her ways. This builds suspense about whether Petersen will keep her.

After using the fictional DecisionTech team to illustrate what dysfunctions are, and how they can be overcome, Lencioni discusses the dysfunctions model he uses as a management consultant. He lays out the five dysfunctions of a team and ways to overcome them in a straightforward way. The presentation is simple enough and clear enough that anyone who wants to apply the solutions to their organization can adopt the model.

PERSPECTIVE

Patrick Lencioni, the author of *The Five Dysfunctions of a Team,* is a well-known consultant, author, and speaker on business management, particularly team building. He is president of the Table Group, a consulting firm whose key areas of expertise include building executive teams and creating healthy organizations. Lencioni developed the concepts in *The Five Dysfunctions of a Team* from his work at the high tech companies Oracle and Sybase, where he was Vice President for Organization Development, and as a management consultant at Bain & Company. He has written eight other business books and a book on how families can manage their activities stress free job.

REFERENCES

1. Gordy, Bill, "Implementing the Japanese Business Practice of Nemawashi," The Solutions Group, accessed October 16, 2015, www.thesolutionsgroupinc.com/implementing-the-japanese-business-practice-of-nemawashi.

~~~~~~~ END OF INSTAREAD~~~~~~~